MARRIAGE: COVENANT OR CONTRACT

by
Craig Hill

FAMILY FOUNDATIONS PUBLISHING
P.O. Box 320
Littleton, CO 80160

Family Foundations Publishing
P.O. Box 320
Littleton, Colorado 80160
Printed in the United States of America

First Printing: 1992
Second Printing: 1994
Third Printing: 1997
Fourth Printing: 1999

CONTENTS

Chapter 1
Covenant vs. Contract   1

Chapter 2
Five Historical Views of   11
Marriage

Chapter 3
Counsel To Single Divorced   23
Believers

Chapter 4
What If I Am Already Remarried   39

Chapter 5
God's Faithfulness To A Covenant   47
Keeper

Chapter 6
Choose Whom You Will Serve   59

INTRODUCTION

"Now therefore, fear the Lord and serve Him in sincerity and truth; and put away the gods which your fathers served beyond the River and in Egypt, and serve the Lord. And if it is disagreeable in your sight to serve the Lord, choose for yourselves whom you will serve: whether the gods which your fathers served which were beyond the River, or the gods of the Amorites in whose land you are living; but as for me and my house, we will serve the Lord" *(Joshua 24:14-15).*

A primary question which I believe Christians have to answer again in the 1990's is, "For whom are you living?" Without having first answered this key question, many other questions of biblical interpretation are simply one person's opinion versus another's. This is certainly the case regarding the issues surrounding the biblical view of marriage, divorce and remarriage.

A man's morality will almost always determine his theology, not vice versa. People first choose how they wish to live and then construct and conform their world view to suit their lifestyle. It is a rare person who objectively looks at the Bible in inductive study to see what is said and then brings his life in conformity with biblical standards. This is no different for Christians than it is for non-Christians.

Unfortunately, Jesus has not really allowed us as His followers this option of conforming our lifestyle to that of society around us and yet continuing to claim that Jesus Christ is Lord.

"Not every one who says to Me, `Lord, Lord,' will enter the kingdom of heaven; but he who does the will of My Father who is in heaven. Many will say to Me on that day, `Lord, Lord, did we not prophesy in Your name, and in Your name cast out demons, and in Your name perform miracles?'

And then I will declare to them, `I never knew you; depart from Me you who practice lawlessness.' Therefore, everyone who hears these words of Mine and acts upon them, may be compared to a wise man, who built his house upon a rock. And the rain descended and the floods came and the winds blew, and burst against the house; and yet it did not fall, for it had been founded upon the rock. And everyone who hears these words of Mine and does not act upon them, will be like a foolish man, who built his house upon the sand. And the rain descended, and the floods came and the winds blew, and burst against the house; and it fell and great was its fall" (Matthew 7:21-27).

I believe that the lifestyles and standards of western society around us are just about as far removed from biblical standards as the Amorite culture was from that of Israel in the days of Joshua. Joshua issued a challenge to the people of Israel to choose whom they would serve. I believe that God would issue the same challenge to us today in the Body of Christ, to choose whom we will serve, either Jesus Christ or self. All of society around us is geared to serve self. The goal of life is "my happiness." Happiness and self gratification are the god that has been served in most of western society for years.

If we say that we are followers of Jesus, that Jesus is Lord, yet continue to embrace the values of society around us, we cause our interpretation of the Bible to conform to standards and values designed to serve self and not God. We are then self-deceived practitioners of lawlessness, who are building our houses upon sand.

In the kingdom of God, happiness is not the goal of life. Obedience to Jesus and the promotion and expansion of His kingdom are the goals. Joy and fulfillment of life are the byproducts of serving Jesus, not the goal. One who seeks the byproduct rather than the goal usually misses out on both. Jesus said that in seeking to save your life you lose the very life you are seeking to save (*see* Mark 8:34-37). So, serving Jesus and serving self are opposites and are incompatible. God has never forced or pressured anyone to choose to serve Him. It is a free choice for us as it was for the Israelites in the days of Joshua. However, we must know that there is a choice to be made. If we say we serve Jesus and continue to embrace the values, standards, and lifestyles of society around us which are contrary to the words of Jesus, then no matter what we say, we have chosen against Jesus Christ and His kingdom. We cannot serve the gods of the "Amorites" and Jesus Christ at the same time. So, CHOOSE THIS DAY WHOM YOU WILL SERVE.

This book is written for those who desire to serve Jesus Christ and to whom serving Jesus means more than life itself. If that is you, read on, as the following material will bring you life and healing. If, instead, the goal of your life is to avoid pain and secure personal happiness, there is no need for you to read further in this book. It will only waste your time and make you frustrated and angry.

CHAPTER 1

COVENANT VS. CONTRACT
(THE PASTOR REPENTS)

Over a period of years, as I was seeking the Lord regarding the issues of marriage, divorce and remarriage among Christian believers, the Lord began to convict me that the standards and goals of our western society are far away from and in many points diametrically opposed to those of the Bible and the kingdom of God. The more I read my Bible and prayed, the more I saw how much my own thinking was conformed to society and not to the Word of God. After much agonizing and prayer, the Lord led me to stand in the pulpit of our church and repent for my own embracing of society's standards and forsaking of Jesus' standards. I held my Bible up before the people and proclaimed, "This book is totally irrelevant to our culture. We must make a choice to embrace either this book or embrace our culture, but one thing we will no longer do in this church is try to squeeze this book into our culture. It simply won't fit."

Mercy and compassion for individuals tend to be very strong motivating factors for me as they are for many pastors. Out of my desire to see benefit and happiness come to individuals in our church, in the first couple years I had participated in many remarriages of people to partners other than the one from whom they were divorced. I had no idea that in so doing, **I was participating in the destruction of our society, releasing a curse on future generations, and embracing values diametrically opposed to those of the Bible and the kingdom of God.**

However, over a lengthy period of seeking God and studying my Bible, the Lord clearly led me to these conclusions. This was no small matter and had serious ramifications for our church in view of the fact that a majority of the congregation was either divorced and remarried, or divorced and single. It was not a particularly exciting prospect for me to share with the church the things I had discovered in the Word of God. However, it was less exciting to consider facing the Lord to explain to Him why I had not.

To make a fairly long story short, I first repented before the Lord and before the congregation for embracing and teaching anti-biblical values, in spite of the fact that much of the church embraces and teaches these same values. I then taught several weeks on what I have come to believe are the biblical values of marriage, divorce and remarriage. Unfortunately, as I suspected might be the case, over the next few months, several individuals and families left our church. However, many others remained whose marriages and lives have been significantly strengthened.

I believe that over the last 150 years in general and over the last 50 years more specifically, there has been a significant exchange of fundamental values in western society. This exchange of values has not only impacted society, but has also permeated the church. The primary value exchange which has impacted our understanding of marriage is that of covenant for contract.

I am convinced that the biblical concept of marriage is that of a blood covenant. Blood covenant is an eastern concept which has been known and practiced for centuries in the east, but is little known, nor understood in the west. The Bible is set in an eastern context, and much of the biblical presentation of God's relationship with man is couched in blood covenant terminology. Unfortunately, most of us in the west have very little familiarity even with the concept of blood covenant. The closest most of us have come to the concept of covenant is watching Geronomo make a blood covenant with another Indian chief on TV when we were children and then pricking our own finger with a friend in order to become blood brothers.

A blood covenant is the closest, most sacred, most enduring, binding agreement known to men. Jonathan and David made such a covenant with each other as recorded in I Samuel 18.

"Now it came about that when he had finished speaking to Saul, that the soul of Jonathan was knit to the soul of David, and Jonathan loved him as himself. And Saul took him that day and did not let him return to his father's house. Then Jonathan made a covenant with David because he loved him as himself. And Jonathan stripped himself of the robe that was on him and gave it to David with his armor, including his sword and his bow and his belt" (I Samuel 18:1-4).

When men made such a covenant with each other, they made a commitment to each other more valuable than even their own lives. When entering into such a covenant, they made the basic commitment to each other that "all I have and all I am is yours. Your enemies are my enemies, and I am ready to give up even my life for you, if need be."

Such a covenant was virtually never broken. It was such a sacred commitment that a man would die before he would dishonor himself by breaking a

3

covenant. In the east, a man's word in a vow or covenant was more valuable than his life. It is said that 100 years ago if a man ever broke a covenant in Africa, even his own relatives would help hunt him down to kill him. He and his offspring would be hunted and killed for up to four generations for covenant breaking. It is said that among North American Indian peoples that a covenant breaker is hunted and killed for up to seven generations.

These types of understandings still exist in oriental and middle eastern cultures today. This is why it is still such a serious matter in many countries for an Arab Muslim to become a Christian. In their way of thinking, the man is in covenant through Islam with God and his brothers. In becoming a Christian, according to eastern thinking, a man is breaking this covenant with God and his brothers and thus is worthy of death. In many cultures, his own mother is sworn to seek his death. Covenant is an irrevocable, indissolveable commitment breakable only by death. Covenant breaking in the east is virtually always punishable by death.

It is an astounding thing that Almighty God would make covenant with man, committing all He is and all He has to us. Jesus Christ took upon Himself the punishment for our covenant breaking in His establishment of the New Covenant and offered to all who will receive an irrevocable, indesolveable covenant commitment.

The concept of covenant then, is a unilateral, irrevocable, indissolveable commitment valid at least until death. Covenant does not depend upon the performance of either party. Covenant is a unilateral commitment made to another party in the presence of

God and is independent of the performance of the other party.[1]

The concept of contract, on the other hand, is an entirely different concept. **A contract is a bilateral agreement between two parties totally dependent upon performance of the agreement.** Under a contract, if one party fails to perform according to the contract, the other party has no obligation to perform either and is no longer bound by the terms of the contract. This is not the case under a covenant which is totally independent of performance and is irrevocable. A covenant was simply not broken, and if it ever were, the penalty was death.

Up until recent years, the concept of marriage, even in society at large, has been that of covenant, not contract. The concept of marriage in Jewish Palestine at the time of Jesus was most definitely that of covenant and not contract. Until recent years the church has always viewed marriage as a covenant rather than a contract.

Unfortunately, over a period of time the unbelieving world, out of an alleged concern for the individual, began to forsake the biblical value of covenant in marriage and instead embraced the value of contract. Much of the church, rather than being the salt and light that it ought to be, has allowed the world to influence it and has ultimately embraced the same values. In so doing we have participated in releasing a massive destructive force in society which is ravaging our marriages and families.

I believe that in marriage this exchange of the value of covenant for the value of contract is responsible for a major portion of the abuse and dysfunction currently taking place in families. Let me explain. The covenant value in marriage would say to the marriage partner, "I am irrevocably committed to you until death separates us. My commitment to you has nothing to do with your performance or any choice you make. It is a unilateral commitment before God unto death." This is the commitment that Jesus made to us. *"I will never leave you or forsake you" (Hebrews 13:5).*

The contract value would rather say, "I'll keep my end of the bargain if you keep yours. If you make me unhappy or don't do what you promised, then I will leave you and find someone else who makes me happy and keeps his/her promises. And if you leave me, then I will definitely leave you and find someone else." Aren't you glad that your relationship with Jesus is a covenant commitment on His part rather than a contract commitment?

I believe that people naturally know what Apostle Paul tells us is true in Ephesians chapter 5:22-33. In this passage, Paul states that a marriage is the primary earthly picture of the relationship between Christ and the church. That means if I want to find out how Jesus relates to me, I ought to look at the relationship between a man and his wife. If, when doing so, the primary value I see represented is the value of covenant, then I would be receiving a correct picture. However, if when doing so, the primary value I see represented is that of contract, then a wrong image of my relationship with Jesus is established in my heart. I don't believe that this is necessarily a conscious thinking process, but the heart naturally embraces the modeling of parents and other significant role models.

It is an even more serious situation when there is no distinction between the values of those called by the name of Christ (Christians) and unbelievers. If believers who ought to represent the values of God embrace the same values as society around them, then there is nowhere to look for a correct picture of relationship. Obviously, the primary impact upon the heart of a child comes through the relationship of his own parents. When a child looks at his parents and sees the value of contract presented in their marriage, it tends to release a tremendous fear of abandonment in the heart of the child. Why?

If the message presented between the parents is that of contract, "If you make me unhappy or don't measure up, I'm going to leave you and find somebody else," the heart of the child thinks, "I wonder what will happen to me if I make him/her unhappy and don't measure up?" In the heart, this feeling is naturally next transferred to God. Even as Paul said, the marriage is a picture of my relationship with Christ. In my relationship with Jesus, the heart conclusion is that I am like my mother and Jesus is like my father, and if I make Him unhappy, or don't do what is right, or leave Him, or am unfaithful to Him in any way, He is going to leave me and find someone else.

This creates a tremendous fear of abandonment even in relationship with God and results in an intense performance orientation and perfectionism in life. "I had better do everything just right and never sin, or Jesus will leave me and find someone else who does things right." Perfectionism and performance orientation are then the root of shame of self and others which results in family dysfunction and abuse. Dr. Sandra Wilson has

7

written an excellent book describing in detail this above mentioned process. I highly recommend Dr. Wilson's book entitled, "Released From Shame, Recovery For Adult Children of Dysfunctional Families".[2]

When Christian parents exchange the value of covenant for contract by embracing the practice of divorce and/or remarriage as a viable option for Christians, they open the door of their children's lives to the enemy and frequently release a literal generational curse. Through the above mentioned process a second generation is set up for family dysfunction in adulthood, frequently leading to divorce, thereby setting up the third generation for the same. This process then continues indefinitely until someone obtains knowledge of the process and chooses to break the cycle.

> *"For lack of knowledge my people perish."*
> *Hosea 4:6.*

Whether they realize it or not, parents hold in their hands a powerful key to the future lives of their children. Parents are the primary agents through whom impartation of image comes to children, either from God or from Satan. The image that I receive in my heart as a child about who I am, who God is and how I relate to Him and others often structures the course of my adult life, as mentioned above. God's primary mechanism of impartation of identity and destiny to people is blessing.

In the Hebrew language, the verb to bless is "*BARUCH.*" One of the primary meanings of this word is *"TO EMPOWER TO PROSPER."* A good definition of cursing, then, would be *"TO DISEMPOWER FROM PROSPERING."* Thus, parents may be used

8

either as an agent of God to bless their children, or as an agent of Satan to curse their children. So, through blessing, parents can literally empower their children to prosper and thrive as adults in their marriages, family relationships, businesses, ministries, health, and finances, while through cursing, parents can mar, cripple, and literally prevent their children from thriving and prospering in all these same areas of adult life. Unfortunately, many of our own parents were deeply wounded and caught in a devastating cycle of cursing themselves before they ever became parents. As a result, many of us received the devil's image of ourselves and God throughout most of our growing- up years.

However, Jesus Christ has come to this earth as a Redeemer to restore to your life and to the lives of your children everything that the kingdom of darkness has stolen. In order to break the cycle of fear of abandonment, shame, perfectionism, dysfunction, abuse, divorce and remarriage, many people need much healing of heart and a deep revelation of the love and faithfulness of God. Through a 3-day seminar we conduct entitled, "**Family Foundations Basic Seminar (From Curse to Blessing),**" I have seen over and over again the Father God impart into peoples' lives His love and blessing in every area where they failed to receive blessing through the default or active cursing of parents. We have also seen the entire lives of young people changed as their parents received understanding of the seven crucial times when children need their parents' blessing. I have seen extremely destructive cycles broken in families as parents have received God's love

9

and healing themselves, have asked their children's forgiveness, and have then blessed their children.

The cry of my heart is that we turn this cycle of destruction and devastation around in this generation, at least among Christians. Let our children not have to bear the pain and devastation that many of us have suffered. Let our grandchildren not have to know the torment of a broken home, abuse, shame, etc. Let this be the generation in which the curse is broken, and God's blessing is released upon our children and grandchildren. (For more information on how you can participate in a **Family Foundations** seminar in your area see page 67 in the back of this book.)

CHAPTER 2

FIVE HISTORICAL VIEWS OF MARRIAGE

I believe that by exchanging the biblical value of covenant in marriage for the cultural value of contract, we as the church have ceased to be salt and light and are participating aggressively in the wholesale destruction of our society and, more importantly, of the image of God in the sight of others.

When did this exchange first begin? It first occurred back in the sixteenth century through a humanist philosopher named Desiderius Erasmus, who had great influence on Martin Luther and other early reformers. Paul E. Steele and Charles C. Ryrie have written an excellent book entitled "Meant to Last" in which they discuss the five historical views of divorce and remarriage including that introduced by Erasmus.[3] I highly encourage you to read this book in its entirety as it is excellent.

In reviewing the five historical views of biblical teaching on divorce, it is interesting to note that there is nothing new under the sun. Most of the so called new revelation and theories that we come up with in modern times were thought of and wrestled with centuries ago. The five historically accepted views of divorce and remarriage are as follows.

1. The Patristic (or early Fathers) view
2. The Erasmian (or traditional Protestant) view
3. The Preterative (or Augustinian) view
4. The Betrothal (or engagement) view
5. The Consanguinity (or unlawful marriages) view[4]

At this point I quote below Steele and Ryrie's description of each view.

The Patristic View
Careful research through the hundreds of manuscripts written by leaders of the first five centuries has revealed that with only one exception (Ambrosiaster, a fourth-century Latin writer), the fathers were unanimous in their understanding that Christ and Paul taught that if one were to suffer the misfortune of divorce, remarriage was not permitted, regardless of the cause.

This remained the standard view of the church until the sixteenth century when Erasmus suggested a different idea that was taken over by Protestant theologians. In the Patristic view, the only reasonable explanation for the disciples' reaction to Christ's words in Matthew 19:10 was that Christ was not following the arguments of the rabbinical schools of either Hillel (divorce and remarriage allowed for any trivial reason) or Shammai (divorce and remarriage allowed in cases of adultery), but was presenting an entirely revolutionary concept---that divorce is sinful and not according to God's plan; but if divorce were to take place, remarriage was forbidden. Great weight was given to the word order of Matthew 19:9 which, the fathers held, forbade remarriage even when immorality was involved.

The Erasmian View

This view of the divorce/remarriage issue is by far the most widely accepted today among Protestants. It holds that Christ's words in Matthew 19:9, allowed divorce in the case of adultery and, since in Jewish marriage contracts the granting of divorce always implied the right to remarry, he also was permitting the innocent party to remarry. *(Author's note: Steele and Ryrie are not here asserting that the granting of divorce under Jewish law did indeed imply the right to remarry, but rather that Erasmus and those following his viewpoint have erroneously tried to make such a case, and thereby interpret the words of Christ.)* Most of those who take this position also say that Paul further expanded this concept by allowing for divorce and remarriage in the case of the willful desertion on the part of the person's partner. Many even go further by allowing divorce and remarriage to take place for a variety of reasons---irreconcilable differences, mental promiscuity, mistreatment, etc.

At the beginning of the Reformation, the classical humanist Desiderius Erasmus suggested this interpretation and it is defended by the modern reformed scholar John Murray. Erasmus was a contemporary of Luther who influenced Luther's thinking on a number of issues but eventually broke with the reformers.

It is curious that though Erasmus was essentially regarded as heretic by his contemporaries, the Reformation writers were greatly influenced by his doctrine of divorce and remarriage. Since most evangelical literature has in turn been influenced by the reformers and subsequently by the Westminster Confession, his view is widely held among evangelicals today.

The Preterative View

This view is not given a great deal of consideration by other than serious scholars, due to its quite complicated exegesis which makes it difficult to explain to the English reader. We are indebted to Bill Heth, who has done extensive research in the subject, for clarifying this view for us.

Simply stated, the Preterative view, promoted by Augustine, holds that the Pharisees were trying to trick Jesus into entering a debate between the liberal school of Hillel and the more conservative school of Shammai, but Christ did not take the bait. Instead He deftly avoided the issue until He was in private with His disciples, where He clarified His meaning (*see* Mark 10:10-12).

The controversy was over the meaning of Deuteronomy 24:1, "some indecency." They asked Christ to comment. The Augustinian view holds that Christ's words "except for immorality" were actually a preterition (a passing over) which bypassed their question altogether. Christ said, "And I say to you, whoever divorces his wife [setting aside the issue of the meaning of 'some indecency'] and marries another woman commits adultery." Then when they were alone with Christ in the house, and the disciples were pressing Him to settle the dispute, He said, "Whoever divorces his wife and marries another woman commits adultery against her" (Mark 10:11).

This seems to cover the cultural possibility that in Roman culture divorce was required in the case of adultery and Christ was in such a case forbidding remarriage. Because the evidence in support of Augustine's opinion is stronger than generally recognized, it is surprising it is so seldom discussed as a possibility in the plethora of popular books on the subject.

The Betrothal View

This view claims that Christ's exception clause (Matthew 19:9) allowed for the breaking of an engagement in the case of a violation of the betrothal terms by the immorality of the party, previous to consummating the actual marriage.

The arguments in favor of this position have merit. When one understands the binding nature of betrothal in the time of Christ, and the clear recognition of the need for a "divorce" to break the engagement (as illustrated by Mary and Joseph in Matthew 1:18-20), one can readily see that such an interpretation is possible. Since engaged couples referred to their fiancees as "husband" and "wife," it is said that for Christ to not address Himself to this possibility would have opened the way to misunderstanding and shut the door on even the breaking of an engagement. The point is made that Christ carefully chose the word "fornication" (porneia) to stand in contrast to "adultery" (moicheia). Both words speak of sexual unfaithfulness, the former to premarital unfaithfulness and the second to marital unfaithfulness.

The Betrothal view, held by a number of evangelical scholars, has much to commend it.

The Consanguinity View

This view, defended admirably in Carl Laney's book, The Divorce Myth, holds that Christ used the word porneia in the specialized sense of the prohibited degrees of consanguinity *(Author's note: This means: marriage between persons of the same blood)* and affinity in Leviticus 18:6-18. Hence a divorce would be allowed in the extraordinary circumstance of being married to a near relative. Apart from this circumstance, neither divorce nor remarriage would be permitted. There is considerable support for this view in Acts 15:20, 29 and I Corinthians 5:1 and in the Dead Sea Scrolls.

The arguments in favor of the Consanguinity view are strong enough that those dealing with the divorce/remarriage problem feel some need to discuss them. But it is disappointing to see them cast the view off as untenable with only cursory comments since, in face, it has wide support in scholarly circles. While it is not without its difficulties (as is true of all five positions), it does have much to commend it.

With divorce being the problem it is in our day, it is imperative that we look for the view that is not just the most palatable to our age, but the one that is most true to God's ideal, most consistent

16

with God's character, and which fits most accurately all biblical data on the subject.

The Question of Remarriage

Before concluding this survey, it may be helpful to summarize what each of these views says about remarriage.

1. The Patristic view disallows remarriage even though a divorce has occurred. This was the Lord's teaching as well as the Apostle Paul's understanding of His teaching. Only two alternatives exist: be reconciled or remain unmarried (II Corinthians 7:11).

2. The Erasmian view, which allows for divorce in cases of adultery or desertion (other reasons are also added today), permits the "innocent" party to remarry without any question. If the divorce is legitimate, this grants freedom to the offended party to remarry.

3. The Preteritive view, while recognizing that divorce may happen, does not permit remarriage.

4. The Betrothal view concerns giving a bill of divorce during the period of engagement before the marriage is consummated in case of premarital unchastity. Therefore, there never was a first marriage, only an engagement. Thus the offended party could enter into a second engagement which, when consummated, would be the first marriage.

5. The Consanguinity view, though recognizing that divorce may have to be instituted in cases of unlawful marriages, considers remarriage of such persons contrary to both Christ's and Paul's teachings. It also holds that in

17

the case of a lawful marriage, divorce is forbidden and the remarriage of a divorced person is never permitted.

Observe that only the Erasmian view permits remarriage. This may account for its popularity today! But it should be noted that even if immorality justifies divorce, the texts in question actually do not justify remarriage. The modernization of the Erasmian view seems to assume that remarriage is automatically permitted if divorce occurs for the permitted reason(s). But this is an exegetical leap of faith!

Today a strained exegesis of I Corinthians 7:15 is used to justify remarriage in cases of desertion of the believing partner by the unbelieving mate. Paul says that the believer "is not under bondage" in such cases. This is understood by modern Erasmians as meaning that the believer is free to remarry. Checking a number of commentaries on this verse, we found that the vast majority agreed that the meaning is that the believer is not bound to keep the marriage together and may have to accept separation if the unbeliever departs. As one suggested, the believing partner "was not bound to chase the unbeliever all over the Roman Empire if the unbeliever chose to leave!"[5]

In Steele and Ryrie's further probing of the Erasmian view they discuss the following:

The Erasmian View
This view, by far the most popular among evangelicals today, seems on the surface to be the simplest to understand and, because of its wide

acceptance, to be the correct one. However, when it is examined thoroughly, it is not so clearly conclusive. And since this is the only view of the five that allows for remarriage after divorce, it is crucial that it be examined carefully.

The logic of the reformers that rose from Erasmus's deep human concern for the individual was this. If one partner committed adultery, he would, according to Old Testament law, be stoned to death. Therefore, it was assumed that the adulterous partner was, "as dead in God's sight," thus freeing the "innocent" party to remarry. This, said the reformers, was behind Jesus' exception clause, and thus the innocent party was free to divorce and remarry whenever immorality was involved.

This idea has been espoused from Luther to the present day. E.J. Ehrlich calls it "legal fiction,"[6] since it assumes the adulterer should be treated "as if he were dead."[7] Because of the obvious absurdity of "legal fiction," many evangelical writers today do not follow that idea, but it is still heard on occasion. The fact is, the person is still very much alive, and a supposed "death" does not negate marriage. Nevertheless, this is the kind of reasoning which popularized the Erasmian doctrine.

Erasmus, a contemporary of Martin Luther, was considered a friend of the Reformation because he spoke out against the abuses of power in the Catholic Church. Luther broke with him, however, because of Erasmus's heretical ideas and his weak view on justification by faith. But for some reason, Luther favored his ideas on divorce and remarriage, thus rejecting the teaching and practice of the early church.[8]

Steele and Ryrie then bring the following comments in conclusion.

Summary

In summary, all five views presented here agree on some basic points.

♦ God's best is monogamy and He hates divorce.
♦ Divorce under the law was a concession to hard hearts.
♦ Christ taught and upheld God's highest standard in His teaching.

The Patristic view and the Erasmian view agree the Porneia may mean adultery. But the Erasmian view is the only one to allow remarriage after divorce. The other views, while recognizing that divorce may sometime happen for various reasons, are unanimous in their conviction that remarriage is contrary to Scripture, and never permitted.

The eunuch saying in Matthew 19 indicates that Christ was not siding with either Hillel or Shammai, but was presenting a concept revolutionary to the minds of the disciples. The Erasmian view ignores this context as irrelevant to what Christ said in the preceding verses. It also fails to explain adequately the clear teaching of Mark 10 and Luke 16, while the other four views see those texts as supporting their thesis that no remarriage is allowed. That also seems the most consistent with Paul's understanding of the meaning of Christ's words as given in I Corinthians 7:10-13.

The believer who suffers the misfortune of a divorce has two clear options: remain unmarried or be reconciled to one's mate. To teach anything else is inconsistent with God's standard for marriage.[9]

I believe that Satan is not only after marriages and families, but is ultimately after the image of God in the sight of people. If he can distort the image of God in the sight of people so that a false image of who God is and how He relates to man is established in the hearts of people, then he can make it virtually impossible for them to truly trust God. I believe that in forsaking the covenant value of marriage and embracing that of contract, Desiderius Erasmus opened the door for the present wave of divorce, dysfunction, abuse, and family destruction which we are now experiencing in the church in the 1990's.

When Christian pastors and leaders authorize and condone the remarriage of divorced Christians, they are aiding Satan in misrepresenting the image and character of God. In our desire to extend short-term mercy and grace to individuals, we are releasing long-term wholesale destruction of our children and grandchildren. We have almost no earthly picture of one who would keep a covenant even in the face of betrayal. Thus a Christian marriage which should portray the covenant-keeping relationship of Christ and His church instead often times portrays covenant breaking, selfishness, and impartation of a deep fear that incorrect behavior will result in rejection and abandonment.

21

CHAPTER 3

COUNSEL TO SINGLE DIVORCED BELIEVERS

In our present society, one of the most difficult tasks for leaders is that of maintaining biblical standards while expressing an understanding concern and compassion for the people who have been ravaged by divorce, abuse, and family dysfunction. I have encountered many Christians who embrace a covenant understanding of the marriage, divorce and remarriage issues, but lack compassion for the individuals concerned.

Divorce and the events leading up to it are very traumatic, and great mercy and compassion are necessary in dealing with those who have experienced such trauma. As I mentioned earlier, it is sometimes difficult to convey the compassion and mercy of the Lord necessary to deal with the hearts of individuals ravaged by this trauma without compromising biblical covenant values. However, this is something pastors and leaders must learn to do. I have copied below much of a letter which I wrote to a divorced man who was seeking a courtship relationship leading toward marriage with a divorced woman. Both of these people were Christians with a heart for the Lord. The names of the individuals have been changed, but the content of the letter is substantially unaltered. In this letter, I have attempted to convey a covenant understanding, recommending that this man either remain single, or seek to be reconciled with his wife.

Dear Jack,

I want to thank you for submitting your proposed courtship of Jill to me for my consideration. I have spent considerable time in prayer regarding this matter and am writing to let you know that I cannot, in clear conscience, approve of your marriage to Jill nor, consequently, your courtship for the following reasons.

1. It is morally wrong and violates the letter, spirit and intention of the Word of God, in general, and more specifically, Jesus' teaching in the Gospels. *"And it was said, `Whoever sends his wife away, let him give her a certificate of divorce; but I say to you that everyone who divorces his wife except for the cause of unchastity, makes her commit adultery; and whoever marries a divorced woman commits adultery" (Matthew 5:31-32).*

When I read the sermon on the mount, it is evident to me that Jesus is contrasting Old Testament standards of behavior with His significantly more restrictive standards encompassing not only external behavior, but also attitudes and motives of the heart. He is commanding His church to live by a much higher standard of conduct than required under the law, not a lower one. Jesus, also under the New Covenant, introduces grace and forgiveness, which were little known under the Old Covenant.

I have heard grace defined as "God's unmerited favor"; however, I find this definition highly inadequate. Upon searching in my Strong's concordance and Vine's dictionary, I found this definition; Grace: "God's empowering presence, exerting a divine influence upon the heart resulting in manifest change in the life." I do not believe that grace grants me the right to do what I want or feel I must in pursuit of happiness or peace, but rather the power to do what is right for the sake of Jesus Christ and His kingdom.

In the above scripture passage, Matthew 5:31-32, Jesus deals with what appear to me to be two entirely separate issues: 1) Divorce and 2) Remarriage. He first speaks about divorce as one matter, and then deals with remarriage of a divorced woman as a separate matter. In your and Jill's lives, divorce is an already accomplished act in which you either sinned, were sinned against, or both. I believe that God's response to this sin is forgiveness, the same as it would be toward anyone who confesses any sin and is repentant (meaning turning from it and having the same hatred for it as God does).

The second part of verse 32 has to do with remarriage. Jesus here states that whoever marries a divorced woman commits adultery. Divorce and remarriage, from what I can see are two entirely separate issues. According to Jesus, for you to marry Jill who is a divorced woman, you would be committing adultery. This you have not yet done, so we are not talking about forgiveness of the past; we are talking about whether or not you should commit a future sin of adultery.

In Jesus' further teaching on this subject in the Gospels of Mark and Luke, He states that for a divorced man to marry not only a divorced woman, but any woman, he commits adultery.

"And He said to them, `Whoever divorces his wife and marries another woman commits adultery against her; and if she herself divorces her husband and marries another man, she is committing adultery" (Mark 10:11-12).

"Everyone who divorces his wife and marries another commits adultery; and he who marries one who is divorced from a husband commits adultery" *(Luke 16:18).*

What I see in these scriptures, Jack, is that for you, a divorced man to marry Jill, whether she were divorced or not, according to Jesus, you would be committing adultery, denying the authority of the Word of God to govern your life and forsaking the Lordship of Jesus Christ.

Some say, "Well, that sounds like legalism. You want to put us under the Law again when by God's grace Jesus set us free." Actually, if we were to return to be under the law, the demands upon our lives in this area are significantly less stringent than that which Jesus' teaching requires. Again, I do not believe that God's grace gives me the freedom to ignore the clear teaching of the Word of God to do what I want in pursuit of happiness, but rather the power to do what is right, perhaps even to my own detriment, for the sake of Jesus Christ and His Kingdom.

I believe that the primary confusion is that somehow many link divorce and remarriage together in the belief that if a man is forgiven for the sin of divorce, or has been sinned against by a divorcing partner, that he is then authorized by "grace" to commit the sin of adultery in remarriage. Jesus makes it very clear that both of these actions are independent sins. Having been forgiven for divorce, in no way authorizes you to commit adultery through remarriage. *"What shall we say then? Are we to continue in sin that grace might increase? May it never be! How shall we who died to sin still live in it?" (Romans 6:1-2).*

As far as I can see, Jack, the issues of divorce and remarriage in your life are similar to the issues of illegitimate conception of a child (perhaps even by rape) and a subsequent abortion in the life of a single Christian woman. Grace requires forgiveness for the sin of fornication resulting in conception of a child, if the woman is repentant. In the case of rape, grace requires great compassion, love and healing to be ministered. However, grace does not sanction abortion because of the forgiveness for fornication or compassion for the rape victim.

Is it legalism when we counsel single, pregnant, Christian women against abortion? Is getting pregnant outside of wedlock an unforgivable sin, for which they must continue to be held accountable? No! Of course, not. But there are consequences of such sin, which are not eradicated by forgiveness, and certainly grace does not authorize abortion. This truth regarding abortion is parallel to that of remarriage. Actually, the Bible, in general, and Jesus, in specific, is much, much clearer regarding remarriage than regarding abortion, about which very little is directly stated. However, we seem, in the body of Christ, to have little difficulty understanding this principle concerning fornication and abortion, and great difficulty understanding it regarding divorce, and remarriage, about which the scriptures are clear.

2.   For you, as a divorced man, to marry Jill contributes to the destruction of the spiritual wall which is meant to protect God's people from the pillaging of the enemy. In order to help bring understanding to this point, I am copying here a portion of a short book I have recently written.

In ancient times, when a significant population settled in one place, and there began to be commerce and accumulation of economic substance, the settlement became ripe for pillage and plundering by neighboring enemy peoples. As a result, one of the first things that was done when a city sprang up was to build a tall, thick wall around it. The purpose of the wall was to keep out enemies. As soon as the wall was in place, and the city was secure, only a relatively small number of warriors needed to stand guard on the wall and repel any sort of marauding enemies. Before the wall was in place, though, everyone had to be a warrior, and much of his time and energy was consumed with concern about enemy activity.

Once a good wall was built, very few enemies were even seen any more. It was much easier to attack a settlement without walls completed than a walled one. After a couple of generations had lived within a walled city, so few enemies ever appeared that many inhabitants had very little awareness of the purpose of the walls. The problem with walls is that they keep inhabitants in just as effectively as they keep enemies out. This can often times be inconvenient.

Suppose a fisherman dwelling in a walled city quite by accident discovers that the largest fish can be caught in a nearby pool only in the middle of the night. However, the gates to the city close at dusk. Since this man lives adjacent to the city wall, he decides to dig a small hole in the city wall through which he can come and go at night. He does not believe that the city is really harmed by his small breach in the wall.

However, one evening one of his friends inquires as to how he is able to catch such large fish. He shares the secret with his friend, who then also digs a small hole in the wall near his own house. You know the scenario from there. Soon everyone who lives along the wall has a small breach in the wall through which he can personally come and go at his own discretion. If we follow this through for a couple of generations, all we have left are a few pillars standing where the wall used to be. It is now very convenient for all the inhabitants to come and go as they please. News of this situation soon reaches enemies who begin to raid and plunder the city again. Now under this circumstance, every citizen is again a warrior. No longer can children play outside alone. Every minor task becomes a life-threatening experience. It is now dangerous to go down the street to buy a loaf of bread, or even go outside to the outhouse at night because of the danger of enemy snipers. The lives of these inhabitants are now consumed with concern for the security of their families and households rather than for the pursuit of the calling and purpose of their lives. This is a physical picture of the spiritual status of our present society. Many of us are so absorbed with the daily maintenance tasks of living in a city without walls that we have no time or energy to pursue or even discover the purpose and calling of our lives.

Suppose, then, that the city council in those ancient times decides to rebuild the city walls. Now the grandchildren of the first fisherman who punched the initial hole through the wall own an entire fishing business employing 100 people who all depend upon fishing at night. When the city council announces that the new wall will extend right across their fishing path, all 100 of these families are up in arms about the idea.

The problem with rebuilding walls is that it always costs very dearly for the generation in which the walls are rebuilt. They are forced to make a choice, either for their own short-term personal benefit, or for the benefit of the entire city and future generations.

"And they that shall be of thee shall build the old waste places: thou shalt raise up the foundations of many generations; and thou shalt be called, 'The repairer of the breach, the restorer of paths to dwell in'" (Isaiah 58:12, KJV).

I believe that God is calling us, in this generation, to be the people who will rebuild the walls that have been made into ruins. We are called to repair the breaches in the walls and to restore the ancient paths of God, not to contribute to their further destruction.

Jack, I have also enclosed, herewith, a copy of some statistics regarding the lives of American children taken from the January, 1991, Charisma magazine. I believe that these devastating events, reported in this copied page, are a direct result of the church in America embracing society's standards rather than Jesus' standards. If you were to make a choice not to be remarried or to work toward being reconciled with your wife, I believe that you would be like one of the fishermen in the above scenario who chooses, even to his own hurt, to support the rebuilding of the wall for the good of the entire city and future generations. I realize that just as it would be very difficult and costly for the men in the above scenario to choose to rebuild the wall and trust God for their livelihood, so it would be for you to choose not to remarry.

ONE DAY IN THE LIVES OF AMERICA'S CHILDREN

Every day in the United States:
   2,795 teenage girls get pregnant
   1,106 teenage girls have abortions
   372 teenage girls have miscarriages
   689 babies are born to women who have
         had inadequate prenatal care
   67 babies die before one month of life
   105 babies die before their first birthday
   27 children die from poverty
   10 children are killed by guns
   30 children are wounded by guns
   6 teenagers commit suicide
   135,000 children bring a gun to school
   7,742 teenagers become sexually active
   623 teenagers get syphilis or gonorrhea
   211 children are arrested for drug abuse
   437 children are arrested for drinking or
         drunken driving
   1,512 teenagers drop out of school
   1,849 children are abused or neglected
   3,288 children run away from home
   1,629 children are in adult jails
   2,556 children are born out of wedlock
   2,989 children see their parents
         divorced[10]

I believe that for us, as pastors and members of the body of Christ, to continue to condone, sanction and encourage divorce and/or remarriage as viable options for Christians may appear, in the short term, as an act of mercy, grace or compassion; but long term, by doing so, we have torn down the corporate wall of protection for our people and continue to refuse to rebuild it. As a result, Christians face choices and situations which God never intended for them to have to face. I would venture to guess, Jack, that a significant reason for your marriage's terminating in divorce has to do with the devastation and wounding that came to you and your wife while growing up. This wounding probably occurred as a result of dysfunction in your and your wife's families due to choices that the last couple of generations made to tear down the wall.

It is neither grace nor mercy for us to continue to opt for the short-term supposed benefit of individual fisherman at the expense of the entire city. Someone, somewhere, sometime, has to begin to make choices for the wall for the good of others, rather than against the wall for the good of self. I realize that it is a costly choice, but I am now appealing to you, Jack, to please consider making such a choice for the sake of Jesus and His Name and for our children, grandchildren and other, as yet, innocent ones, whom the enemy desires to ravage through our refusal to rebuild the wall of protection. I really do believe that the Kingdom and the lives of others are at stake in these decisions, just as much as is true regarding abortion. Abortion is also a choice for self and against God and others. The only difference is that we directly see at least one person whose life is immediately impacted by abortion, namely that of the murdered baby. We don't always see who is impacted by our choosing for our fishing business and against the reconstruction of the wall.

If the primary reason that you feel that you could not reconcile with your wife is that she has not yet received the healing necessary to make her suitable to be a wife, please consider waiting for her and exercising faith for her healing and/or deliverance. She could not be worse than the Gadarene demoniac out of whom Jesus cast a legion of demons as recorded in Mark 5. In verse 19, Jesus told the delivered man to go home and report to everyone what great things God had done for him. **If the story were told in modern times, it would then record that the delivered man went home only to find that his wife had divorced him and remarried someone else.**

3. For you to remarry severely devalues marriage and makes it common rather than holy. It also testifies to the world that the Bible has no authority in the lives of Christians, and that the church holds the same values as the world and has lost its salt (*see* Matt. 5:13).

I believe that the primary issue here is the defamation of the image and name of God in the sight of others. As the body of Christ, we bear the image of God on the earth to others around us. Unbelievers look at the body of Christ to see who God is and what He is like. When we, as the body of Christ, embrace the values of society around us rather than Jesus' values, we defame the character of Christ in the sight of those around us and become a stumbling block and hindrance to their salvation.

God speaks in Ezekiel 36:17-33 that His primary motive in giving His people a new heart and putting His spirit within them was not for their sakes, but for the sake of His Name.

"When they came to the nations where they went, they profaned My holy name, because it was said of them, `These are the people of the Lord; yet they have come out of His land.' But I had concern for My holy name, which the house of Israel had profaned among the nations where they went. Therefore, say to the house of Israel, `Thus says the Lord God, "It is not for your sake, O house of Israel, that I am about to act, but for my Holy name which you have profaned among the nations where you went"'" (Ezekiel 36:20-22).

I do not believe that God is speaking this way to Israel because He is condemning and judgmental. He is not saying that He has a concern for His Holy Name out of pride or self adulation. I believe that He speaks this way out of love and mercy for all concerned. His Name represents His character, and when it is defamed by His people in the sight of those who do not know Him, then they are stumbled and hindered from knowing Him. This is the concern for His Name.

Again the issue is not sin, repentance nor forgiveness. It is not sin that defames the name and character of God. The heart of God for people requires the church to love, accept and receive people in whatever condition they may come to us, regardless of what they have done. When people in the church sin, it is not our job to wave the Bible in their faces, judge them and condemn them "to uphold God's name." This attitude also defames the name and character of God in the sight of others. I believe that when people sin, we are called to love them, accept them, instruct them, call them to repentance, forgive them when they do repent, and take them on in God. This is the process that I believe represents the heart and character of God.

So, my concern for the name and character of God in the present matter is not sin and forgiveness, but rather the church's embracing of values which are contrary to and in direct violation of those expressed by Jesus in the Bible. When we in the church, in the name of "grace" toward an individual, at the expense of the whole body, embrace a value which we can statistically see is devastating people in our society and is contrary to God's Word, then we are participants in defaming God's name in the sight of others.

In Ephesians, chapter 5, Paul tells us that marriage is an earthly picture of the relationship between Christ and His church. I believe that a fundamental value behind marriage is the concept of covenant. This is why marriage is a representation of Christ and the church. God has made a covenant with us by the blood of Christ. When we marry in our society, most people still use covenant language, a remnant of the prior biblical concept of marriage as a covenant rather than a contract. The minister usually states something to the effect that marriage is an institution sanctified by God, and he calls it "holy matrimony." It usually includes most of the constituents of a formal blood covenant. There is a greeting, a charge, vows unto death are made to one another, external tokens of the covenant (rings) are exchanged, witnesses are present, and it is usually sealed by blood (not our own, but the blood of Christ in communion) and names are exchanged.

In our society, we (including much of the church) have exchanged the biblical value of covenant in marriage for the value of contract. The difference, as I understand it, is as follows: Covenant is a unilateral commitment valid until death. It does not depend upon the actions of the other party. According to what I have read regarding how covenant has been practiced and still is among those who do so, once having made one, a man would die before breaking one. This is my understanding of Christ's relationship with His church. A contract, on the other hand, is a bilateral agreement between two parties consummated by an offer and acceptance, breakable by non-performance on the part of either party.

When we, the church, exchange God's value of covenant in marriage for the world's value of contract, and teach that this is right to do in the name of "grace" toward individuals, we are defaming the name and character of God, misrepresenting the relationship of Christ with His church, and releasing into society in general, and the church in specific, a tremendous insecurity and fear of abandonment. I know from speaking with other pastors and from experience in my own ministry that one of the biggest problems we deal with in the lives of our people today is insecurity and the fear of abandonment. Christians, by and large, are not convinced that God has their best interest at heart and that He is committed to them in covenant (by the blood of Jesus) and not by contract (dependent upon their performance). I believe that this is a direct result of our forsaking God's value of covenant in marriage and embracing the world's idea of contract.

I realize that we are now two or three generations into this exchange of values and are now reaping the consequences in terms of tremendous dysfunction in present marriages whereby people do great damage to one another in relationship. Many times marriage partners must be separated from each other for the purpose of mitigating damage to one another and to bring about healing. This may be for a relatively short time or it may be a long time. However, if we in the church, because we want people to be "happy," encourage such a person to forsake covenant, embrace contract and simply go and find someone else with whom to enter into a new contract, we are perpetuating the problem of misrepresenting the character of God and relationship of Christ and His church. This results in insecurity and fear of abandonment that produce shame and dysfunction which perpetuate transgenerationally and produce the fruit of abuse, codependency, control, manipulation, etc. In my opinion, somewhere, sometime, someone has to begin to look beyond the individual to see what we are doing to families and people long-term through our short-term choices for the happiness of the individual.

All through the Bible, I find examples of people willing to forsake their own individual happiness and comfort for the sake of others and the kingdom of God. I realize that this is not something that can be legalistically put upon someone, and I am not advocating that Christians embrace the attitude of a "noble martyr" for Jesus. However, I would appeal to you, Jack, to consider the longer term consequences of your choices upon your own children and the rest of the body of Christ. Please consider embracing and upholding the value of covenant in marriage, even if it means living the rest of your life as a single man if you are never reconciled with your wife. I realize that I have not walked in your shoes and have not experienced what you have experienced, so I cannot evaluate, from your perspective, what I am appealing to you to consider, but I do know that God is just and kind and that should you choose to uphold the covenant image of Christ by remaining single or working on reconciling with your wife that you will not be disappointed and that God will more than make up for whatever loss you experience.

Thank you, Jack, for hearing my heart on this matter. I felt that it was important for me to explain to you, in some detail, why I cannot approve of your courtship of Jill. I have a deep love for both of you and whatever choice you make will not change the fact that you are my brother in Christ and I love you and want God's best for your life.

Your brother in Christ,
Pastor Craig Hill

CHAPTER 4

WHAT IF I AM ALREADY REMARRIED?

Many people say, "Well, I'm divorced and am already remarried to another partner. What about me?" As I mentioned in the above copied letter, there are two areas of sin to be dealt with in this case: 1) Divorce and 2) Remarriage. Covenant breaking is the primary issue of which there must be repentance. Covenant breaking occurs with divorce for the initiating partner. It occurs for a "victim" or recipient of divorce at the time of his/her own remarriage. Jesus calls this adultery. From my study of the Bible, I believe that the adultery that Jesus is speaking of is the act of remarriage, not the ongoing sexual relationship between the remarriage partners. This sin of remarriage then must be dealt with just as is any other sin, through repentance and forgiveness.

As I mentioned in my letter quoted in the last chapter, remarriage to another person can be likened to abortion. Until there is repentance and agreement with God there is always a lingering guilt and condemnation in the heart. Are divorce and remarriage unpardonable sins? No more so than fornication and abortion. However, a woman will never be free from the guilt of having had an abortion as long as she continues to justify this sin and claim that it was the right thing to do. The same is equally true regarding remarriage.

Remarried couples have often told me, "We wouldn't repent of our remarriage because we are convinced that God led us to be married. We have overwhelming confirmation that it was God's will for us to be married." Of course it is very difficult to dispute a couple's personal testimony regarding what they thought they heard from the Lord.

However, I know that as recorded in the Bible, Jesus Christ calls remarriage adultery. *"Everyone who divorces his wife and marries another commits adultery; and he who marries one who is divorced from a husband commits adultery"* (Luke 16:18). Therefore, we have two statements diametrically opposed to each other. We have one who says that God led him/her to do that which Jesus clearly categorizes as "committing adultery". Since God would not lead a person to sin (commit adultery), I can only conclude that one of the opposing parties was deceived and misinterpreted the will of God, either the remarried person, or Jesus.

Obviously, it was not Jesus that missed the will of God. However, I realize that this is very often a very difficult thing for a remarried couple to accept emotionally. It was devastating enough to pass through the emotional trauma of divorce, but to now recognize that the Word of God calls remarriage adultery is very difficult to handle initially.

Unfortunately, in our desire to be led by the Spirit, we in the body of Christ have exalted and placed more weight and emphasis on our subjective experience of the Lord's speaking to us than what is clearly stated in the Bible. This leads people to "pray" about clearly stated biblical precepts. When we do this, we open ourselves to deception. I have encountered Christians who have told me that through prayer they were led by the Lord to engage in an adulterous affair. Subsequently, these same ones have been "led by the Lord" to divorce their marriage partner and marry the other person. We, as Christians, don't need to pray about whether or not to rob a bank, steal a car, have an affair, abort our babies, or divorce our spouse and marry another. These matters are clearly dealt with in scripture. To pray about such things almost always leads to deception. You will always hear a voice asking you, "Has God really said?" and stating, "He didn't really mean that." Nothing has really changed since the serpent in the garden spoke similar words to Eve.

As I mentioned in the introduction to this book, a man's morality will almost always dictate his theology. People first choose how they wish to live and then construct and conform their interpretation of scripture to suit their lifestyle, not vice versa. It is a rare person who has the integrity and trust toward God to objectively read the Bible to see what is said and then conform his/her life to the Word of God no matter what the cost.

Frequently, because of the way Christians have been treated in the past by parents, pastors and other spiritual leaders, when they have sinned or made mistakes, the fear of rejection, shame and punishment has become a very powerful force in their lives. This fear is often projected toward God resulting in a remarried couple's justification of their wrong choices rather than agreement with the Word of God and repentance. The truth is that God is not like any other person that we have ever met. When God deals with us, it is always out of love, and He always has our best interest at heart.

Every time I have seen a remarried couple acknowledge the sin of their divorce and of their remarriage, repent of these sins, forsake their justification of it, and come into agreement with God regarding it, there has been a new freedom which has come into their relationship. This repentance has then released forgiveness and cleansing to come by the blood of Jesus. As long as a person continues to disagree with God, and justify that which is wrong, obviously there can be no cleansing and forgiveness, as the blood of Jesus is being trampled under foot (*see* Heb. 10:26-29).

Humility, agreement with God, and repentance bring forgiveness, release from guilt, cleansing, healing, and blessing. If you are remarried and have come to recognize that your remarriage constitutes the sin of adultery, I would like to lead you in the following prayer of repentance and forgiveness.

"Father God, I thank You that you love me and are for me, not against me. I repent of the sin of divorce. I agree with You. Divorce is wrong. Please forgive me. I recognize that I have been a covenant breaker and have committed adultery through the sin of remarriage. That was wrong. I repent of covenant breaking and ask You to forgive me, cleanse me and remove all guilt from me. Lord Jesus, thank You for shedding Your blood for me. I now receive Your forgiveness and commit myself totally to You. I acknowledge that I am not my own and that I am no longer living for my own personal happiness and self gratification. I choose to live from this time forth for Your kingdom, Your Name's sake, and Your image in the sight of others, no matter what that might personally cost me. Forgive me, Lord for having treated marriage as a contract and I ask You for Your grace to empower me to be a covenant keeper from this point forward. Amen."

When there is no former faithful marriage partner believing God for the restoration of the former marriage, and there is genuine repentance and forgiveness for the sins of divorce and remarriage, I believe that we could view a subsequent marriage of previously divorced persons as a covenant much like that which was made between the Israelites and the Gibeonites as recorded in the book of Joshua, chapter 9.

God had instructed Joshua and the Israelites to eliminate from the land all the Canaanites living there. They had already totally annihilated the cities of Jericho and Ai. They were now nearing the Hivite city of Gibeon. The Gibeonites had heard what had been done to Jericho and Ai and were greatly frightened. The elders of the city devised a plan to deceive Joshua and induce him to enter into a covenant of peace with them. They knew that if they could get the Israelites to enter into a covenant with them, they would then be bound to do them no harm.

The Gibeonites sent an envoy to the Israelite camp with worn-out shoes and clothing, stale bread, and cracked and mended wineskins to make it appear as if they had traveled a very great distance. They arrived and appeared before Joshua in this condition and sought to enter into a covenant of peace, saying that they were not inhabitants of the land of Canaan, but rather lived a very great distance away. Joshua and the elders of Israel did not seek the counsel of the Lord, but rather believed the Gibeonites and cut a covenant of peace with them. Only three days later, Joshua discovered that the Gibeonites had deceived him and were occupants of the land of Canaan. Although all of Israel would have liked to destroy the Gibeonites, Joshua and the leaders prevented them because of the covenant which was made with them.

Despite the fact that it was a covenant that was never meant to be and even was entered into through fraud and deception, once it was made, the Israelites were bound to honor it. Joshua and his leaders understood the issue of covenant and its value before God. They could not break their covenant even though it was made in deception with heathen Canaanites whom God had commanded the Israelites to destroy.

Joshua's concept of covenant was so strong that not only did he preserve the Gibeonites, but in Joshua chapter 10, he and the Israelites fought alongside the Gibeonites to help defeat their enemies. God so honored the value of this covenant that He placed it even above the individual welfare of His chosen people Israel. In II Samuel chapter 21, a famine had been released upon Israel. When King David inquired of the Lord as to the famine, the Lord informed him that it was a result of King Saul's having violated the covenant and putting the Gibeonites to death. The famine was terminated only as King David went to the Gibeonites and repented and made restitution for the rebellious acts of former King Saul. We see here again the incredible value God places on covenant as He honors a covenant that should have never been made in the first place.

So it is with many second marriages of previously divorced people. Jesus calls remarriage, adultery, and it should never take place. However, if it does, just as with any other sin, *"If we confess our sins, He is faithful and righteous to forgive us our sins and to cleanse us from all unrighteousness. If we say that we have not sinned, we make Him a liar, and His word is not in us" (I John 1:9-10).* If there is no faithful, covenant keeping former spouse and there has been an acknowledgment of sin, agreement with God, repentance and forgiveness, then I believe that God will honor and bless even a covenant which was expressly forbidden, just as He did with the Gibeonites.

CHAPTER 5

GOD'S FAITHFULNESS TO A COVENANT KEEPER

Over the last couple of years I have become aquainted with a remarkable woman, Marilyn Conrad, who has lived through the tragedy of divorce and has chosen not to remarry, but rather to remain faithful to her marriage covenant and to rebuild her life in Christ. Following is an account of Marilyn's experience.

"In January, 1980, at 4:30 in the morning my husband announced that he was leaving and he wanted a divorce. From my bedroom window I watched him back our car out of the driveway, tears streaming down my face. Devastated, I dropped to my knees and asked God to do two things: I asked Him to start with me and show me where I had failed and needed to change, and then I asked for the help I needed to heal my marriage.

My husband and I had been married for 27 years. We had one son in college and another who had just graduated from high school. As a pastor-evangelist my husband was well known, loved and respected in our denomination.

I began to search the Bible for God's will on divorce and remarriage. I knew that I had vowed before God to, `love, honor and obey until death do us part,' but did I have a right to remain committed when my husband wanted out? Was there nothing I could do to turn this around? Did

47

his free will override God's will? In other words, would it really do any good to pray?

I studied the scriptures for the next two weeks and then read a book on intercession. By the time I laid the book down I knew that I had the covenant right to stand in the gap for my mate. I saw that I was not praying against his free will, but as I did spiritual warfare I was pulling down strongholds over him, so he could hear from God. When he heard from God his will could line up with God's will.

I dropped to the floor and began to pray and intercede for my husband, claiming God's word. Having just recently received my prayer language, I began to pray in tongues. Then a strange thing happened, just like the book I was reading had described. I began to groan and travail. It was as though what I was doing with my mind dropped down into my spirit. Although my mind didn't understand what was happening, in my spirit I understood that the Holy Spirit was praying God's perfect will for my husband (*see* Rom.8:26-27). When I got up off the floor, I knew that I knew that I knew, that my marriage was healed regardless of the circumstances.

The Lord took me to Hebrews 11:1; *"Now faith is the substance of things hoped for, the evidence of things not seen."* I had substance in my spirit for the healing of my marriage, even though I could not see this happening in the natural. The written word of God, the logos, had become a word from God to me, personally. It had become rhema to me. The "said" word had become a "saying" word. In the months and years ahead I would come to realize how important this was. When God speaks, no one can take this substance from you. When you or others begin to question because circumstances aren't changing, you can return to what God spoke to you in the beginning.

I soon discovered that when we stand in faith for something, God often times gives us the beginning and the ending, but He doesn't give us the middle. Perhaps He knows we would probably give up! Habakkuk 2:2-3 says; *"For the vision is yet for an appointed time and it hastens to the end (fulfillment) it will not deceive or disappoint. Though it tarry, wait [earnestly] for it, because it will surely come; it will not be behindhand on its appointed day."*

So I began to walk out my "tarrying" time. The first year was a healing time for me. The Lord taught me the importance of forgiveness and that it is a process. Time after time He taught me that forgiveness was a choice I had to make: an act of my will, regardless of how I felt. He showed me that forgiveness meant giving up my right to hurt. As I forgave my husband, I opened myself up to the healing power of Jesus Christ.

As the healing process continued, Jesus began to do a deep work in me. He began to show me my own heart. I saw that I was self-righteous and legalistic and that these spirits and attitudes had to go. Matthew 7:3-5 says; *"And why worry about a speck in the eye of a brother*

49

(mate) when you have a board in your own? Should you say, 'Friend, let me help you get that speck out of your eye,' when you can't even see because of the board in your own? Hypocrite! First get rid of the board. Then you can see to help your brother." Another way of saying this is, "Let God do a work in you, so He can do a work through you."

I stood and believed that the divorce would not go through; that my husband would change his mind. He didn't though and the divorce was granted. Although disappointed, I knew that a man-made decree could not break my covenant. I saw that I could not box God in, and that He was determining if I really would trust Him to do what He promised, regardless of the circumstances. I learned that I could not be moved by what I saw, what I heard, or what I felt. I must keep my eyes on Jesus. 2 Cor. 4:18 says; *"We look not at the things which are seen but at the things which are not seen, for the things which are seen are temporal (subject to change) but the things which are not seen are eternal."*

Matthew 19:6 says; *"So, then, they are no longer two, but one flesh. Therefore what God has joined together, let not man separate."* When a partner, out of obedience to this command, develops a stand of faith and holds the covenant, a divorce decree does not end the covenant in the spiritual realm before God. In the earthly realm, we recognize the divorce and realize that we give up the privileges of being married. Man-made decrees and their outcome can be changed through fasting and prayer. The example God gave me is in the book of Esther when the Jewish people fasted and prayed and God turned the heart of the king. A decree that ordered the killing of all the Jews was canceled and instead became a source of victory for the Jewish nation.

Next, something happened which most people would interpret as God closing the door. My husband remarried. Immediately, I went to the Lord and asked, "Where did I miss it? You told me my marriage was healed." In my spirit I heard, "You didn't miss it, daughter. My word prevails over this situation also." Then I heard the word "annulment."

So I went back to God's word. In Matt. 19:9 Jesus says, "And I say to you, whoever divorces his wife, except for sexual immorality, and marries another, commits adultery; and whoever marries her who is divorced commits adultery." Although the remarriage was legal in man's eyes, Jesus called it adultery.

So I quietly continued to stand and hold my covenant. I used wisdom and discretion in discussing my situation with others and continued to let God do a work within me.

One day while praying, I saw (in the spirit) my husband sitting in his car in front of a tall building. I heard the words, "He knows what he has to do and he is making plans to do it." I continued to pray, and two months later he had the marriage annulled. I then discovered that what I had seen that morning when I was praying was my husband in front of the lawyer's office.

Our first grandchild was due at this time, and every day I had confessed, "Our grand baby is not coming into a divided, broken home." The morning the birth announcement appeared in the daily newspaper, right beside it was the annulment of the non-covenant marriage. Because I truly believe there are no losers in these situations, I continued to pray for the other woman for a year. Then, one morning the Lord released me. I later heard from a friend that she had repented and admitted that the marriage to my husband was wrong from the beginning.

I expected my husband to return to me and our family. However, instead, he soon married for the second time since our divorce. At this point I really needed encouragement! In my spirit God was saying that He would use my situation to help the Body of Christ to understand the non-covenant marriage, and that He would give me the grace to walk it out.

The Lord then spoke to me through Ezra 9 & 10. In chapter ten, verse three God, through the priest, Ezra, instructed 113 men to divorce their non-covenant wives and return to their covenant marriages. *"Therefore let us make a covenant with our God to put away all the foreign wives and their children, according to the counsel of my Lord and of those who tremble at the command of our God; and let it be done according to the law."* The Hebrew word used for foreign wives (nokriy) is defined in Strong's Concordance as "adulterous" wives.

Ezra and Malachi were prophets who ministered during the same period. The tears shed in Malachi 2 were shed by the covenant wives who trusted God to restore their husbands to their rightful places. *"And this you do with double guilt; you cover the altar of the Lord with tears [shed by your unoffending wives, divorced by you that you might take heathen wives], and with your own weeping and crying out because the Lord does not regard your offering any more or accept it with favor at your hand" (Mal. 2:13, Amplified).*

My husband's relationship with this woman lasted only four years. In the end, both wanted out. It was mutually agreed upon to get a divorce.

During this time I had opened my home to others who were going through separation and divorce, individuals committed to the permanency of marriage. Like me, most had discovered abundant counsel on divorce and making new lives for themselves, while finding a lack of help or encouragement for reconciliation and restoration.

I began to share with them the things God was teaching me on a daily basis. For example, the Lord spoke to me early one morning as I got up to water the lawn. After moving the sprinkler, I knelt down and started pulling up weeds in the area that had just been watered. While doing so, I heard the Lord say, "I have something for you to share with your group. Did you notice how easily the weeds came up?" I said, "Yes, Lord." He said, "That's because you had watered the ground. That's what happens when you pray My word over your mates. You are watering them with My word. Be faithful to confess My word over them and then the strongholds will come down easily."

It was also during this time that I made a wonderful discovery about the principles in God's word regarding sowing and reaping. Genesis 8:22 declares that while the earth remains, seed time and harvest will not cease. In the New Testament Gal. 6:7 tells us; *"Be not deceived, God is not mocked. For whatsoever a man soweth that shall he also reap."*

I had always been a tither, but now I entered into the joy of giving above the tithe into the needs of others, personally and through my church. Although I was not giving to get, the wonderful result was that my own needs were met abundantly.

I found that this principle of sowing and reaping not only pertains to finances, but also to many other areas of life. As I began reaching out to other hurting people, I stopped hurting. When love and forgiveness were given, I experienced love and forgiveness from others. When I needed prayer, I prayed for others. When I was lonely, I found another who was also lonely and ministered to him or her. Because of the law of increase (one seed produces many seeds), the fruit was always much greater than what I had sown. I was reaping a harvest. One definition of harvest is: the consequences or products of any effort, action or event. When we give, God has something to multiply back. When we withhold, God has nothing to increase.

Psalm 112:3 says; *"Wealth and riches shall be in my household."* One morning I asked the Lord to teach me what He meant by this verse. I looked up riches in the dictionary and found that it meant: 1) abundant possessions; wealth 2) abundance of whatever is precious (like a healed marriage).

Next, I looked up wealth. The definitions were: 1) a large aggregate of real and personal property; 2) an abundance of those things men desire: riches; the state of being rich. (The next meaning caught my attention!) 3) great abundance of anything, usually preceded by a wealth of learning.

When I first began believing God for the healing of my marriage, I wanted a miracle immediately. "Bring my mate home NOW! Heal my marriage NOW!" Proverbs 5:1 says that wisdom is learned by "actual and costly experience." As I was willing to walk out my miracle moment by moment, hour by hour, day by day, week by week, and even year by year, I was gaining actual and costly experience. I was gaining a wealth of learning, and I ended up with a ministry to broken marriages. I am indeed a wealthy woman!

It has now been over 13 years since my husband first left, and I am more convinced than ever that it is right for me to uphold my marriage covenant and believe God for the healing of my marriage. Recently at a Prophetic Conference at our church, my son and I received the laying on of hands with prophetic words from the Lord. The same man, who knew neither my son nor me, gave us *both* the same word.

My son was told, "We all know the story of the prodigal son, but in your case it's reversed. It's the prodigal father and he's coming home. He's coming home!" I was told, "You have waited for years and a miracle is taking place. God is going to move upon this man and you and your whole household are going to see the salvation of the Lord. Your mourning shall be turned into dancing."

God is faithful and I know He will perform His word and bring to pass what He spoke to my spirit in the beginning of my stand. He will perfect that which concerns me and my family. Generational curses of adultery and divorce are now broken over us and covenant commitment is being modeled for our grandchildren who will grow up knowing that marriage is a covenant witnessed by God, "until death do us part.""

Marilyn is indeed a rare woman of honor. I have met very few Christians whose choices are governed by Jesus and His word rather than by the choices of other people. Marilyn's choice to either remain single or be reconciled to her husband has not been impacted by any decision her husband has made, including his remarriage. Very few people, even Christians, live their lives by absolute principles rooted in God. Most meander through life simply allowing the choices of others to determine their own decisions and destiny. Marilyn is truly one of the heroes of the faith in our time.

CHAPTER 6

CHOOSE WHOM YOU WILL SERVE

I realize that we have not in this book touched some of the really difficult issues such as physical and sexual abuse in a family, homosexuality, alcoholism, AIDS, and other severe marriage maladies. When such extreme dysfunction exists in a marriage or family, it must be dealt with swiftly and decisively and frequently through the intervention of others. Unfortunately, these matters are outside the scope of subject matter for this book. **However, even in such extreme situations, the upholding of covenant commitment and the exercise of faith toward God have often proven to be the keys to deliverance, healing and restoration of the individuals, marriage and family.** Covenant breaking through divorce and remarriage, though frequently promoted in the church, are not options for those to whom Jesus is Lord, and who have chosen to live for Him and His kingdom rather than for self and personal happiness.

The primary issue in the question of divorce and remarriage for Christians is not personal happiness, but covenant breaking. The primary issue in covenant breaking is the destruction of the image and defamation of the character of God in the sight of others. This gives rise to a deep seated distrust toward God and fear of abandonment in the hearts of participants, children and other observers, resulting in perfectionism and performance orientation in order to be accepted and not abandoned.

I believe that there are two primary institutions on the earth which bear the image of God. These are: 1) Marriage, and 2) The church. These two institutions are meant to depict to children and the world around who God is and what He is like. In His prayer for the church recorded in John 17, Jesus prayed the following:

*"...that they may be one, just as We are one; I in them, and Thou in Me, that they may be perfected in unity, that **the world may know that Thou didst send Me, and didst love them** even as Thou didst love Me" (John 17:22b-23).*

In the above passage, Jesus states two reasons why the church must be one: 1) That the world may know that the Father sent Jesus, and: 2) That the world may know that the Father loves them. Conversely, when the church is divided, it is a bold statement to the world around us that the Father did **not** send Jesus and that the Father does **not** love people.

We as believers cannot live only unto ourselves. Jesus' concern in this passage is not only for believers, but even more so for others before whom the church is a representation of the image of God. No one individual is the representation of the image of God, but rather it is the collective relationship between believers that bears the image of God. When the church is not one, it is difficult to convince people that the Father loves them and that He sent Jesus Christ.

In the same way as the church bears the image of God, so does marriage. Marriage was not man's idea. It is an institution of God. As I mentioned earlier, in Ephesians chapter 5, Apostle Paul tells us that the marriage relationship is an earthly picture of the relationship between Christ and the church. When there is covenant keeping within a marriage, the image of Christ and His bride is correctly presented before the world. However, when there is covenant breaking within a marriage, the world is presented with the wrong earthly picture of Christ and His bride.

Because marriage does indeed bear the image of God in the world, **both divorce and remarriage are bold statements to those around that the Father does not love them and that the Father did not send Jesus.** I have proven this out in practical experience when attempting to minister to the children of divorced and/or remarried couples. It is very difficult to convince these children that they are truly loved by God and that He really has sent Jesus to die for them. Often deep inside are feelings of unworthiness, shame, and a need to behave perfectly in order to receive God's love and acceptance. They have great difficulty believing that Jesus Christ is committed to love and accept them according to His covenant with them, independent of their behavior. They have never seen modeled covenant commitment independent of behavior. Through the selfishness of parents, Satan has, in such children, effectively set up the next generation to experience the same, if not worse, trauma and devastation in their own lives and families.

We would not expect the world, those who don't know Christ, to uphold God's standards or really to even have a concern for the image of God in the sight of others or for future generations. However, we would expect the church to do so. Unfortunately, among many believers, this has not been the case. The world has been salt to the church, rather than vice versa.

Many Christian pastors continue to remarry divorced Christians to people other than their spouses, thus embracing the world's value of contract, rather than upholding God's value of covenant. I realize that the concept of right and wrong is not particularly strong in our society any more, even among Christians. However, just the fact that this practice **might** be morally wrong (and I believe it is), **might** violate God's will and purpose, and at best is scripturally questionable **ought to be enough to cause pastors to discontinue the practice**.

If the questionable morality of the practice were not enough, we ought to look at the fruit of what we are producing. Family dysfunction and abuse are as rampant and growing a problem in the church as they are in the world. Statistically, divorce among Christians is the same as (maybe even slightly higher than) among non Christians. One would think that the gospel of Jesus Christ would change lives and families and positively impact these statistics. If the fruit produced is not as expected, it would stand to reason to check the seed sown. Either the gospel has no long-term effect on peoples' lives, or we are not preaching the gospel, at least relative to these issues.

In conclusion, I believe that how we answer the following key questions, as Christians, determines how we interpret scripture and view marriage, divorce and remarriage.

1) **For whom am I living? For Jesus Christ, His kingdom, His Name, and His image in the sight of others? Or, for myself, my happiness, and my emotional well being?**

2) **Do I embrace the biblical value of covenant in marriage or the world's value of contract?**

I believe, as Christians, we must answer these questions and live consistently with our choices. If we choose to live for self and personal happiness, we are free to do so, but let's not continue to say that Jesus Christ is Lord and misrepresent His name and image to others. If we choose to value our subjective experience above the written Word of God, then let's just say so and not claim that the Bible has authority in our lives. If we believe that marriage is a contract rather than a covenant, then let's act accordingly and not perform the ceremony as though it were a covenant before God, using covenant language such as "until death do us part" and other such phrases which are really not consistent with a contract belief.

If, on the other hand, we choose to live for Jesus Christ and His kingdom, let's recognize that this may be an extremely costly decision for some who have been ravaged by abuse or divorce. We, the church, must provide them with the love, compassion, mercy, and support they need to make it through the trauma and continue on with Christ. If we believe that marriage is a covenant, then let's uphold the value of covenant within the church and make sure that we impart this value in advance to Christians who are being married. Only let us choose, on purpose, which values we embrace and live consistently with our choices.

"Now, therefore, fear the Lord and serve Him in sincerity and truth; and put away the gods which your fathers served beyond the river and in Egypt, and serve the Lord. And if it is disagreeable in your sight to serve the Lord, choose for yourselves whom you will serve: whether the gods which your fathers served which were beyond the River, or the gods of the Amorites in whose land you are living; **but as for me and my house, we will serve the Lord"** *(Joshua 24:14-15).*

RESOURCES

1) *Rebuilder's Guide*, published by Institute in Basic Life Principles, Box One, Oak Brook, Ill. 60522.

2) *Marriage Ministries, Int'l.*, P.O. Box 1040, Littleton, Co. 80160, phone: (303) 730-3333.

3) *Covenant Keepers*, P.O. Box 702371, Tulsa, Ok. 74105, phone (918) 743-0365.

FOOTNOTES

[1] H.Clay Trumbull, *The Blood Covenant,*(Kirkwood, Mo.: Impact Books, Ink., 1975)

[2] Dr. Sandra Wilson, *Released From Shame,* (Downers Grove, Ill.: Intervarsity Press, 1990)

[3] Paul E. Steele and Charles C. Ryrie, *Meant To Last*, (Wheaton, Ill.: Victor Books, 1986)

[4] ibid., p.88.

[5] Used by permission. Quoted from Paul E. Steele and Charles C. Rryrie, *Meant To Last*, (Wheaton, Ill.: Victor Books, 1986), pp 89-94.

[6] R.J. Ehrlich, "The Indissolubility of Marriage as a Theological Problem," *Scottish Journal of Theology,* August 1970, pp.291-311. Protestant View of Divorce and Remarriage," , Vol. 1, No. 1, 1981, pp. 23.

[7] Bill Heth, "A Critique of the Evangelical Protestant View of Divorce and Remarriage," *Studia Theologica et Apologia* (3909 Swiss Ave., Box 1030, Dallas Texas 75204).

[8] op. cit.,Paul E Steele and Charles C. Ryrie, p.104.

[9] ibid., p115.

[10] From: The Almanac of the Christian World, pg. 779, Edited by Edythe Draper, (c) 1990 by Edythe Draper, Used by permission of Tyndale House Publishers, Inc., All rights reserved

Marriage Ministries International - new phone number (303) 933-3331

You won't want to miss the:
Family Foundations Basic Seminar (From Curse to Blessing)

What Is It?

An intensive time of teaching from God's Word, followed by sharing, prayer, and ministry in small groups. As teaching topics are brought up, the small groups give opportunity for ministry in that specific area of the individual's life, marriage, or family. The seminar is conducted in a Thursday evening, Friday evening, and all day Saturday format.

Topics include:

Communication
> Recognizing different levels of communication.
> Resolving Conflicts.

Purpose and Plan
> Overview of God's plans and purposes for the individual and family.

Identity and Destiny
> 7 Critical Times of Blessing.

Life Patterns
> How to walk in the spirit.
> Impact of lack of blessing or the cursing of identity.

Curses and Blessing
> Releasing God's Blessing to your children and others.
> Practical steps to freedom from cursing.
> Personal Ministry.

Vision Of the Family Foundations Basic Seminar

It is our vision and purpose to help reimpart back into the culture of the body of Christ, those safeguards which facilitate the natural impartation to people of identity and destiny from God. Without such, the devil has been allowed to impart his message of worthlessness and purposelessness to millions of people throughout the earth.

Who should come?

Anyone desirous of lasting change in your life. Many times we see unpleasant, or unhealthy patterns in our lives, but don't know why they are there and/or can't seem to change. This ministry is designed to identify root causes and bring lasting change to these areas.

For a schedule of future seminars or for information on how your church can schedule a *Family Foundations Basic Seminar*, please mail the attached form or call, or fax:

Telephone: (303) 797-1139   Fax: (303) 797-1579

Please send me information about the seminars.

Name   _____

Address   _____

City, State, Zip   _____

Telephone   _____

Mail to:

In North America
Family Foundations Int'l.
P.O. Box 320
Littleton, Colorado 80160
(303) 797-1139

In Europe
Family Foundations Int'l.
P.O. Box 52
Rugeley, Staffs.
WS15 3YZ England

In Australia and the Pacific
Family Foundations Int'l.
4 Prunus Place
Caloundra, Queensland 4551
Australia

TAPES

RESTORING GOD'S ANCIENT WAYS (21 TAPES)
$95

Why is life so complicated in the 1990's? It seems we have to read books just to understand how to do simple existence type of things, like raise families, play or eat properly. Craig Hill says, "It ought not to be that way!" In this series he lays out how God established His ways from the beginning of time and how we are to walk in them.

MARRIAGE: COVENANT OR CONTRACT (6 TAPES)
$30

Marriages in the 1990's are being ravaged by a cycle of abuse, dysfunction, and divorce. Much of this is attributable to a value exchange in society from that of covenant to that of contract in marriage. In this book, Craig Hill outlines how this destructive cycle can be broken through a return to the biblical value of covenant in marriage. This series also includes a dynamic message by Marilyn Conrad, founder of Covenant Keepers.

BLOOD COVENANT (6 TAPES)
$30

"A stranger to the covenants of promise is one who is in the covenant, but doesn't know what a covenant is, or know the provisions or promises of the covenant." In this series, Craig Hill informs you of what a covenant is and how to experience the power of your blood covenant with God.

RELATIONSHIPS (4 TAPES)
$20

When we get to heaven we may find a sign above the throne of God saying, "People are our business, our only business!" Craig Hill shows us how finding God's answer to the identity questions, "WHO AM I? WHO IS GOD? WHO ARE THOSE AROUND ME?, can help us relate to God and others.

JEZEBEL SPIRIT (2 TAPES)
$10

It dominates, manipulates and controls. It makes mighty prophets fearful and discouraged. Its purpose is to divide families. Craig Hill exposes the operations of the Jezebelic spirit and reveals how to war against it and tear it down.

IDENTIFYING SHAME (3 TAPES)
$15

"Every compulsive habit is shame based." In this series, Craig Hill tells what Shame is, how others (especially family) put shame on you and how to get shame off of you.

THE HEART (8 TAPES)
$40

Craig reveals in these tapes that through the loss of ancient values, families break down. The results are devastation and hardening of THE HEART. He also shows us how God can soften the hardened heart and re-establish the covenant with us.

BOOKS

THE ANCIENT PATHS - Craig Hill
$7

No matter your age, God intended for you to feel loved and have a deep inner knowing of who you are and where you are headed in life. Because our lives are so consumed with survival and maintenance activities, many of us will never experience our true identity or really fulfill our God-given destiny until we rediscover.....THE ANCIENT PATHS!!

DECEIVED, WHO ME? - Craig Hill
$9

Since most Christians intend to live life in the Spirit, when we walk in the flesh, it is usually by deception. Deception, by its very nature, is hidden from the person in whom it is working. Often God's intentions for our lives are thwarted by the serpent in our own flesh rising up to deceive our mind, will and emotions, compelling us to walk in its ways and fulfill its plans.

This book is designed to expose the hidden ways of your flesh and to set you on a course of freedom to walk in the Spirit and experience God's purpose and plan for your life.

MARRIAGE: COVENANT OR CONTRACT - Craig Hill
$4

Our modern society has gotten away from the plan that God has for marriage. Is marriage a contract or covenant? Craig Hill examines the scripture for answers.

71

HELP! MY SPOUSE WANTS OUT - Craig Hill
$8

A must read for anyone separated from a spouse, or experiencing marital crisis. Although this book provides immediate help and answers for those with serious marital difficulties, it will also greatly benefit anyone in search of solid, no-nonsense principles and values upon which a lasting marriage can be built.

BONDAGE BROKEN - Craig Hill
$4

In this book, Craig Hill gives you practical keys to break the bondage in your life and release you from the prison of controlling habits. You will discover root causes of bondage and how to tear down strongholds in your life to release you into the peace and joy that God has intended for your to experience.

I'M A NEW CREATION? - Craig Hill
$1.50

Have you wondered why it is that even though you have committed your life to Jesus Christ, you don't always feel or act like a new creation? In this book, Craig Hill gives you practical answers to this question from the Word of God.

YOU DON'T HAVE TO BE WRONG TO REPENT - Craig Hill
$1.50

This is what God told Craig Hill once while he was in the middle of a power struggle with his four-year old son over a hamburger. How can this be so? Pick up this little booklet and in under an hour you will see that you don't have to be wrong to repent.

For a current catalog of books and tapes by Craig Hill and other Family Foundations authors and speakers, please write:

<u>In North America</u>
Family Foundations International
P.O. Box 320
Littleton, Colorado 80160
Tel. (303) 797-1139
Fax (303) 797-1579

<u>In Europe</u>
Family Foundations International
P.O. Box 52
Rugeley, Staffs.
WS15 3YZ England

<u>In Australia and the South Pacific</u>
Family Foundations International
4 Prunus Place
Caloundra, Queensland 4551
Australia